Selected Poems

With the compliments of the Canada Council

Avec les hommages du Conseil des Arts du Canada

LOUIS DUDEK

Selected Poems

THE GOLDEN DOG PRESS
Ottawa, Canada
1975

© Copyright Louis Dudek

ISBN 0-919614-16-7

The Golden Dog Press gratefully acknowledges the assistance accorded to its publishing programme by the Ontario Arts Council and The Canada Council.

CONTENTS

Making Poems 1
Night Scene 2
Late Winter 3
Tree in a Street 4
The Tolerant Trees 5
Clouds 6
Skyscraper Window 7
Puerto Rican Side-street 8
Building a Skyscraper 9
The Pomegranate 11
The Pineal Gland 12
The Cage 13
The Race 14
A Cornet for Critics 15
The Layman Turned Critic 16
Poetry for Intellectuals 16
A Lost Art 17
This Changing World 18
In Days to Come 19
Pure Science 20
Old Song 21
No Answer 22
R.I.P. 23
An Air by Sammartini 24

from EUROPE
The sea retains such images 25
Across the level fields of France 26
A city is a kind of ship 27
The commotion of these waves, however strong 28

I do not think that we shall ever again   29
The present is all too present   30
Where the sea smashes   31
Under the rocks at Biarritz   33
But I had not known the sea would be this splendid   35

from EN MEXICO
Here where the sea washes   36
Stars I have never seen before   37
Order remains unimpaired   38

from ATLANTIS
How seagulls know what they are!   39
Speaking of coral, the white whirling wave   40
Today we passed over Atlantis   41
Marble is the cross-section of a cloud   42
But I have been in a marine aquarium   43
Have you seen the weeping beech   46
Ah, Wyndham!   47
In the daylight of departure   48
To die, to drown, to be free   49
We must go   50
Nothing   51

Les Répétitions   52
Alba   54
Brightness   55

Making Poems

Hanging over a rail of the harbour bridge,
knocking mud
out of the corners and angles of shoes,
diverting traffic
I am walking full of poems; I make them
hitting home runs, taking the sun,
worrying, looking at people.
I am breathing under the excitement.

Night Scene

I meant to be walking in the night-time,
But I lean here, for the street is quiet.
It is very still between the buildings.
No one passes.
Somewhere I hear the notes of a piano,
And into my head drift the words of a poem
Which a while ago I was reading.
I notice how the light from a window
Falls upon the snow in the alley;
The street is quite deserted.
Now a man passes,
Making no more sound than a shadow.
Above me a few stars quietly
Stay between the dark houses.

Late Winter

The sky is scrubbed clean,
      the chimneys stand like springtime sticks
growing out into a world done over.
A fresh lacquer of rain
      dries on the tree branches.

      But the sun is stony
on the houses, on walls of factory metal,
on the tops of buildings
      distinct as in a mortuary.
On the distant roofs it lies cold
like platinum, that the waste
      cotton clouds have polished.
Nature stiffens
      her water-tints in times like these,
makes morals out of her fairy-tales.

Tree in a Street

Why will not that tree adapt itself to our tempo?
We have lopped off several branches,
cut her skin to the white bone,
run wires through her body and her loins,
yet she will not change.
Ignorant of traffic, of dynamos and steel,
as uncontemporary
as bloomers and bustles
she stands there like a green cliché.

The Tolerant Trees

Some conspiracy of silence among the trees
        makes the young birds secret,
or laughing at our infirmities
        in birdlike fashion, they titter in feathers;
but the uncondescending trees,
too wise to speak against us, against streamlining,
        against new fashions in uniforms and clothes,
wear always the same drab leaves,
        preserve a Sachem silence
toward our puberty rites of golf and war.

Clouds

Pale from the storm's mouth
the white clouds move out,
they slowly turn
like hills of clouded ice
or winter glass before our eyes.
Under their shadows burn
battered buildings ashamed,
tenements under East River
under a project of new homes;
the flapping fringes of the city
cower and cover their knees and bones.
But the clouds are not sad
on this account. Can it be that,
somewhere, they see beyond
mountains and green lands?
They move like the Greek philosophers,
wreathed in smiles,
as if the knowledge of love
and timeless peace made them mild.

Skyscraper Window

At the ice-bright window,
if you let the light
dazzle you with silver blisters from
the hump-backed cars, that crawl
aching, in rows
to a green light,
and if you look
down canyons, into distant boroughs
where at last they die like proboscidians
among the ivories and striated marbles
of St. James street,
you may wonder if history
ever knew, or would have been surprised;
if in the streets, the cries
and the coughing in corners,
and the falcons fluttering with blood-stained beaks
could have been foretold
for our pity and amazement,
and whether the nerves we learn by,
teeth, and veins, are tough enough,
and weaponed
to break alive into the green beyond.

Puerto Rican Side-Street

Morning came at me like a flung snowball,
the light flaked out of a chalk-blue sky;
and I was walking down the dilapidated side-street
like a grasshopper in a field, just born;
all the rails and pails glistened and deceived me
with bunches of blue flowers and with silk of corn.

The yellow shades were mostly down, some up, some torn;
and I went looking into windows, into rooms,
looking for the breakfasters, and the cluttered dressers
and cracked walls; watching the black doorways and the dim
charred halls, for the baby carriages and the kids;
and as I walked, they came, like shots in a foreign film.

And then, in a blue window, lifted like a cross,
her legs straight, hair flat, and arms strung wide,
gazing out at the daylight out of coal-black
glassy eyes, I saw the twelve-year child—a saint
upon a stained-glass window—with her blue sash dress
hanging on her, thinly, and her small face thin and faint.

As I passed looking at her eyes held far away,
she almost turned; but the sun suddenly came
from behind some chimney stack, and I went ahead:
the street blazed up again. The morning hour,
that made the ashes shine and the stones burst out in flame,
had shown me in her face the sad, dark human flower.

Building a Skyscraper

By the street's noise muffled, the hammers
sock silently; a mittened hand
plucks concrete pieces from the ground,
throws them with a curse without a sound,
as automatic these men
building a skyscraper in the precincts of Wall street
work without being heard, without headlines, with only
a truckful of sand making rapids of applause.

Skyscrapers have their origins in the Stone Age.
Under the concrete feet of every hall,
under steel, this hammering must be done. So pausing for the bow,
these partners, prototypes of mankind consider
the hole they have made, a place to open a pail, unwrap paper
and eat ham, a cave this winter—but a bone-heap
of vapour and people next summer, a skyscraper.

And here is surprise and paradox; one of the boys
leaning on a handle sports a pipe, is no longer primitive:
the stem is silver, and a luxury of billows
expands from the bowl!
Now he folds on his belly over a steam-drill
and shakes like dead meat—but to him stones give way
and walls fall; he kicks them to hell and the crane,
makes room for a girder, for a small finger
to hold up an iron web in the air,
metallic bones hung in the velvet night,
and clothed with flesh, a hand between the moon and
    men's eyes.

The same man may rivet as well as work a drill,
may measure the dimensions, or draw a blueprint,
approve the designs and pay the bills:
but for a name and a number the same man
plans a city, and builds it, and writes it a religion.
We are identical in everything but words and clothes,
the track we took from the unequal springboard of the womb.

Tomorrow I will come and watch their progress.
I know for certain that these digging men
nudging each other with their elbows, pushing the drill left,
scoop clay from under the rump of profit and finance.
Digging here and in the next street, today or tomorrow,
something will finally happen, a bank will sag,
a building sway like a fork on a prong;
with shouting and throwing from side to side, the houses
will fall into the diggers' arms. The Stone Age will be done.

And then, a colosseum will be made of the street,
sidewalks will become benches, and windows break with cheers.
We will praise "Men Working." They will be celebrated
more than millionaires, since without rich men
nations can run as well, or better, but not without these men.
And because they now work inaudibly, cursing behind a fence,
I know that someday, over the applause and clamour
of the crowd, will fall on every ear the workman's hammer.

The Pomegranate

The jewelled mine of the pomegranate, whose hexagons of honey
The mouth would soon devour but the eyes eat like a poem,
Lay hidden long in its hide, a diamond of dark cells
Nourished by tiny streams which crystallized into gems.

The seeds, nescient of the world outside, or of passionate teeth,
Prepared their passage into light and air, while tender roots
And branches dreaming in the cell-walled hearts of plants
Made silent motions such as recreate both men and fruits.

There, in a place of no light, shone that reddest blood,
And without a word of order, marshalled those grenadiers:
Gleaming without a sun—what art where no eyes were!—
Till broken by my hand, this palace of unbroken tears.

To wedding bells and horns howling down an alley,
Muffled, the married pair in closed caravan ride;
And then, the woman grown in secret, shining white,
Unclothed, mouth to mouth he holds his naked bride.

And there are days, golden days, when the world starts to life,
When streets in the sun, boys, and battlefields of cars,
The colours on a bannister, the vendors' slanting stands
Send the pulse pounding on like the bursting of meteors—

As now, the fruit glistens with a mighty grin,
Conquers the room; and, though in ruin, to its death
Laughs at the light that wounds it, wonderfully red,
So that its awful beauty stops the greedy breath.

And can this fact be made, so big, of the body, then?
And is beauty bounded all in its impatient mesh?
The movement of the stars is that, and all their light
Secretly bathed the world, that now flows out of flesh.

The Pineal Gland

The pineal gland, that was once an eye
on the skull's prow,
dreams now over bales of brain
behind the brow—
dreams of the sea it once knew
when it was young,
and in the darkness still as brave
rocks over thought as on a wave.

The Cage

Conditioned to the cage, my bird,
whose door is always open
has the whole house to himself
but sits always on his small trapeze, within,
or on top, on wires,
and must be chased off with a stick, forced
to take freedom,
protesting with his loud cantankerous cries,
then back, as soon as danger is over,
to his wire cage, a slave
of first comforts, the fictions defining life
and its limits, fiercer than truth.

The Race

Pine trees that grow 200 feet in the air
and have no green but a bunched Christmas tree
    at the top

have done it through competition
with other trees,
like the armaments race,
    or skyscraper cities,

each trying to get the light from the other,
until all are too far from the earth
to get enough juice,
and suck it a half-mile up
    for a mere living.

A Cornet for Critics

The beauty of being a critic
is that one can write as if one were infallible
and be forever wrong

For if one makes a howling error
of judgment such as casting talent
aside, or throwing obloquy
on genius, or praising an ass

one can forget, later, like one's readers

and praise what one called a bore
as infallibly as before.

The Layman Turned Critic

Seeing an elephant, he sighed with bliss:
"What a wonderful nightingale this is!"

And of a mosquito he observed with a laugh,
"What a curious thing is this giraffe."

Poetry for Intellectuals

If you say in a poem "grass is green,"
They all ask, "What did you mean?"

"That Nature is ignorant," you reply;
"On a deeper 'level'—youth must die."

If you say in a poem "grass is red,"
They understand what you have said.

A Lost Art

The trouble with theatre is
that the most dramatic moments of life
are wordless.

The novel, on the other hand,
has more words than anyone can say
in a mere lifetime.

The true proportion exists
in the poem of course.

This Changing World

When the last Pope is dead, and the Vatican crypts are open, there will be—

    after
    2000 years
    of
    obfuscation,
    inquisition,
    forging of documents,
    burning,
    miseducation,
    threats,
    persecution
    and
    prohibition—

A Girl for every boy, and a Boy for every girl (guaranteed by the state).

In Days to Come

Every little girl will know a wasp
can cause a swelling,
and every little boy may dream a room
of plush and apples.

All in a bucket will lie
                the miscellaneous oysters.

But gulls couple-cooing
two by two,
be inseparable, true.

Pure Science

Poetry is a man-made kite
        skating on an imaginary sky,
But nobody knows what the sky is
        nor why there are kite-makers.

It is also like grandmother's idea of heaven
        that we have learned to do without
Because nobody cooks there,
        sleeps with girls, or mints money.

It is a whirling
        spark in a vacuum,
And only scientists seem to
        enjoy the experiment.

Old Song

Since nothing so much is
as the present kiss
don't let an old kiss
so disconcert you,
but know it is no crime
to give a new kiss time
and reason to convert you.

The first you ever had
was an eternal lad
whose smile was very May
no other mouth replaces,
but this today
has an October way
to harvest his embraces.

Loves are the fruits of time
different and the same
the perfect and imperfect,
and in the body's branches
where old kisses hang
and sweet birds sang
the wind fills his paunches.

And any kiss at all
is present after all
for now is all we have
now when we want them,
so grant your kisses leave
to give and to receive
nor waste your lips to count them.

No Answer

A woodpecker knocked on my skeleton
    And found it very hollow
      And very thin
    Where all my aching marrow
      And blood had been.
Then he gave a rap and hopped
    To the crown at the top.

'Knock-knock! Who's there?' he spelled.
    'Tis I,' my soul replied.
      Then he with skill
    Hopped down and looked inside,
      Cleaning his bill
On my nose (or where it once was)
    With a wink and a pause.

'Ho ho!' said he. 'What's this? Are you there?'
    He cocked his head and clicked.
      'How's tricks, mon cher?
    I see you've been cleaned and picked
      Something rare.
But can you hear it still in that box
    When your knees knock?

Ha ha!—in that box, when your knees knock!'
    I looked at him through my jaws
      And my empty eye,
    And got angry, and I was
      About to reply—
When he saw an apple tree
    And whistled away.

R.I.P.

How do you think we'll rest
With tombstones on our chest?
I had rather recline
With your breast on mine,
    Love, on violets.

Or how shall we know peace
Broken piece by piece
In decay? I'd rather fret
Now for what I get
    From lips like these,

And leave nothing to wish
When we've become a dish
For the worms, my friend.
Leave them, hot heart, at end
    Cold cuts to finish.

An Air by Sammartini

It was something you did not know
        had existed—by a dead Italian.
Neither words nor a shape of flesh
        but of air;
                whose love it celebrated
                and "cold passion"
Amoroso Canto, a crystal
        that fell from musical fingers—
As a cloud comes into the eye's arena,
      a certain new tree
             where the road turns,
    or love, or a child is born,
            or death comes:
Whatever is found or is done
        that cannot be lost or changed.

from *Europe*

The sea retains such images
        in her ever-unchanging waves;
for all her infinite variety, and the forms,
inexhaustible, of her loves,
she is constant always in beauty,
        which to us need be nothing more
            than a harmony with the wave on which we move.
All ugliness is a distortion
of the lovely lines and curves
        which sincerity makes out of hands
            and bodies moving in air.
Beauty is ordered in nature
        as the wind and sea
shape each other for pleasure; as the just
know, who learn of happiness
        from the report of their own actions.

Across the level fields of France
extensive as empire or continent
        the wind over the wheat
runs in delicate timid waves, moonlit in daytime.

They cultivate every acre
        with geometrical exactitude
as they built their cathedrals with grace.
        We found this true.

The beautiful mind of the cultivated Frenchman
        must be like these fields, these waves,
an undulation measured like the dance
        of Cleopatra's body.

A city is a kind of ship,
most of it an old tramp
most of it salt-eaten
sea-stained, encrusted
with lives beyond recall;
some of it new
decked with modern apartments
flying flags and bunting
for life's excursion pleasures;
much of it freight and trade.

A city is a kind of ship,
it touches the ports of time—
Past and Present—the wharves of space
—Here and Now—it comes and goes
making its long voyage
and then sinks in the sand:
Troy, Ecbatan, buried cities.

    The commotion of these waves, however strong, cannot disturb
                    the compass-line of the horizon
    nor the plumb-line of gravity, because this cross coordinates
                    the tragic pulls of necessity
    that chart the ideal endings, for waves, and storms
                    and sunset winds:
    the dead scattered on the stage in the fifth act
    —Cordelia in Lear's arms, Ophelia, Juliet, all silent—
    show nature restored to order and just measure.
                    The horizon is perfect,
    and nothing can be stricter
    than gravity; in relation to these
                    the stage is rocked and tossed,
    kings fall with their crowns, poets sink with their laurels.

I do not think that we shall ever again
have great buildings. Temples and churches
built to please or placate a god
were once the occupation of a whole society
led by that superstition. The private dwelling,
or edifice of utility, no matter how pretentious
      —the Pitti Palace, Chambord, Versailles—
is always an atrocity,
      like a much-bejewelled dowager.

Can we find a new symbol
for all those processes
of which we are still a part?
Not until we have become perfectly accustomed
to the invention of elementary machines.

The present is all too present
and the past all too past:
streetcars and Roman crowds, a monstrous static
        of old echoes and new noise.
I cannot hear my own heartbeat,
how should I hear what falls
from the columns of the Twelve Gods
or the hoarse whispers that grow like moss
on the stumps of the Rostra?
Rome was not built in a day, but a day is enough
once it is over, to make an end of Rome.
Nothing has power that was only power
when it lived and had its will; only the power
that is married to beauty survives. Virgil was not satisfied
with his epic when he died, nor Marc Aurelius
        that he was wise.
We may learn from this how the hours should be adorned
        with leaves
and the columns of days garlanded.

Where the sea smashes
        on the rocks at Bordighera:
simply for pleasure,
        like the surf at Sete,
               alone, for miles and miles
        of wind and sea-washed
                        sand

a strip of land, where there is water on both sides
and a good road running by the sea—
lonely, we stopped and stripped
for the sweet salt surf, the sea
        that took us in as though we were nothing
               (making that poem)

or on the glittering Riviera
        (hard pebbles, but good water)
where there are 30 miles also devoted entirely to pleasure,
we rested at any rate, one afternoon
               and slept there
(the Casino stupid and vulgar,
one could see the money
        raked in by the croupier,
and very little coming back)
or at *baccarat*, each betting against the other,
        the House always collecting its dividends.

No art out of this, says Ezra,
there is no art where there is theft on the community
and each bets against the other.
No art in St. Raphaël,
        Nice or Cannes,

a hundred years later, 200 years later
these villas will lie in ruin
still an eyesore
        & the money and the bankers
                        no more
(says, or might say, Ezra);

        but we enjoyed it
        lying on the beach there and sleeping
        after Spain, the fiesta,
        after the ruins of Villafranca,
                      the caves of les Baux,
                              vineyards, the grape country
of Spain and France, equally good
                and the small towns of Provença.

Lay by the sea sleeping
with the Casino overhead,
        and the sea lapping quietly at our feet.

Under the rocks at Biarritz
where the sea rushes in, in terraces
                of white breakers
toward the tourists scattered on the crisp spattered sand—
the two protagonists of this epos,
                the latter creating
hotel fronts
& zebra umbrellas
as usual;
the sea carving the architraves of the ragged rocks.

Beauty is a form of energy.

When that is depleted, pleasure
            or comfort, is all that the organism desires.
The apparent energy of the factories
            and industrial sites, so ugly,
              which we have seen in France and in England
                    (the length and breadth of them)
is really exhaustion, not power, so far as the worker
      is concerned, in his dismal dwellings;
despair because there is no beauty.
And the masters of that system, whom we can now see, if we
      want to,
              will be brutal beings, desperate
in their ignorant search for enjoyment and power;
they cannot be dedicated
or happy in the expression
            of their virility,
nor feel in their veins the sea as they work.
Hence the rich are great drinkers
of hard liquor, and come to these resorts
wearing short trousers,
having shaved their legs cleanly,
their arms like coffee.
They sit confidently
in deck chairs, or under tents
listening to the tame ocean,

        while all Europe is a heap of ruins
covered over with new buildings; new voices
          fill the air where the hammer
chipped the rock once, the bell tolled
serenely. We take the spray on our faces
          like tiny tears
from that great duct which is green and golden.
Can you hear?
The sea is angry, because they have deceived her
          and lied to her.

But I had not known the sea would be this splendid
                magnificent lady:
"destroyer of ships, of cities"
in luxurious ermine and leopard coat
                sighing in the ship's wake;

destroyer of civilizations, of pantheons,
to whom Greece and Rome are only a row of white breakers
spilled with a hush, in air,
then marbled patterns on a smoother wave...

And I would not be surprised if the sea made Time
in which to build and to destroy
as it builds these waves and indolently breaks them,
                or if the whole fiction
of living were only a coil in her curvature
                of immense imagination.

Maker and breaker of nations, sea of resources,
you have enough here for a million rivers,
                for a billion cities,
enough for new Judea, for new Alexandria,
and Paris once again, and America's morning.

from *En Mexico*

Here where the sea washes
                the uneven shore
(down with the slush, up with the blue water)
the white success is one unbroken line from here to Caleta.
Rolled in a long green hollow,
the sea moss thrashes in the brine, and sand bubbles
or glistens with calcareous triumph
                (*now! now! now!*)
and the men bring sea-shells to their wives,
and young girls flash their stiff buttocks
as the sun strikes the winning nipple—
now! say the strings in singing consummation
we have touched the life-giving current,
                making a relay!
Take it from us, you swarming futures!
Sing, as we now sing!

Stars I have never seen before, in the southern sky,
and clouds the colour of roses, of brown trees,
and the *copa de oro* when sun sets
                    in the far sky...
I've gazed at the Great Way,
            there is no end to creation.
Cost what it may,
the petals of the infinite flower
            and time loves their sweet bouquet.

Study the way of breaking waves
for the shape of ferns,
                fire and wind
for whatever blows or burns.

Someday we shall come again to the poem
as mysterious as these trees,
            of various texture,
leaves, bark, fruit
(the razor teeth so neatly arranged,
so clean the weathered root).
There is the art of formal repetition
and the art of singular form—lines clean
            as a wave-worn stone.

Lizards chucking under the eaves.
Vultures among the leaves.
The comical pelican. The plunging fish.
The coconut used as a dish.

Study the ancient habits
of the most disorderly people.
Where did reason arise?
The science of cleanness—
fastidiousness in art?
Somewhere in this, the market, the church,
            the commissary.
No matter how steamy the jungle,
small leaves are perfect in detail.

Order remains unimpaired
in man and in matter,
despite all poverty, insanity, and war—
                  the jungle, in its excesses.

From wherever you are, begin!

To the peak of Popocatepetl
seen in the liquid sky
            (as we came from Taxco)
cutting the air with white precision.

So like the virile leaping of goats
        in a green valley,
love's restorative power
                  leaps to the heart.

Form is the visible part of being.
We know the logic of its adaptations,
a signature of individuality, of integrity,
the end of perfect resolution—
but not the inner stir.

Rest. Rest in that great affair.

from *Atlantis*

How seagulls know what they are!

So to be, whatever you are—
    a white bird,
           a man with a blue guitar.
But there is room for more, more.

It is the part of us
not yet finished as seagull or man
that worries us at the pit of creation,

hanging over cliffs, drowning,
          or lifted in flight

to new states of being, asking always what we are.

Speaking of coral, the white whirling wave
behind the ship
is like a Japanese painting of a wave.

It is not the painting that is like a wave
but the wave like a real painting—
as exact, as detailed, as white and delicate,
made of many tiny hands, of drops, of lacing lines,
a continuous flocculation of white light
that is unlike mere water as a Rembrandt is unlike mere paint.

That nature is the prime artist does not mean that
                      all nature is art.
The means are wasteful, but the occasional fragment
may be a masterpiece, a poem, or even a man.

Today we passed over Atlantis,
             which is our true home.
We live in exile
waiting for that world to come.

Here nothing is real, only a few
             actions, or words,
bits of Atlantis, are real.

I do not love my fellow men
             but only citizens of Atlantis,
or those who have a portion
of the elements that make it real.

One day at sea, at sunset,
             when the long rays struck the water,
it seemed to me the whole sea was living
             under the surface motion;

the waves moved like a great cosmic animal
twisting and turning its muscular body
under the grey glistening skin.

And I thought that land also is such a body,
and all men, and all living things—
the life within made invisible, or hardened,
             or covered with deep hard crust,

until it is scraped or dug for, or cleared away,
or with love reached, or by art or other good,
             seen for a moment—

like a great cosmic animal, of great power, of great beauty.

Eidolons, visions of that reality
             in moments of illumination,
are the things we love.

Marble is the cross-section of a cloud.
What, then, if the forms we know
                are sections of a full body
whose dimensions are timeless
                and bodiless, like poems,
whose unseen dimension is mind?

I want to learn how we can take life seriously,
      without afflatus, without rhetoric;
to see something like a natural ritual,
          maybe an epic mode unrevealed,
in the everyday round of affairs.

But I have been in a marine aquarium and I have seen

        LOLIGO VULGARIS
        TRACHINUS ARANEUS
        SCORPAENA SCROFA
        SCYLLARIDES
        ANEMONIA SULCATA
        ASTEROIDES CALYCULARIS
        MAJA SQUINADO
        MUSTELLUS LAEVIS
        THALASSOCHELIS CARETTA
        TRIGLA CORAX
        TRYGON VIOLACEA
        HYPPOCAMPUS BREVIROSTRIS
        SPIROGRAPHIS SPALANZANII
        ACTINIA CARI
        MURAENA HELENA
        SYNGNATUS ACUS
        RETEPORA MEDITERRANEA
        PELAGIA NOCTILUCA
        PARAMURICEA CHAMALEON

Of a very graceful undulant movement
    of a pale white colour
        with translucent fins

Fish that lie buried in the sand, on the sea bottom,
    with only their eyes peering out

Or long and thin as a pencil
    flexible in movement

Or absurd, barnacled, monstrous bulldogs of the deep,
    and sea-spiders of gigantic size.

Red flowers of the sea
        (or orange coloured)
    like carnations, like broken pieces of pomegranate

(I too was once a fish
I rubbed myself on the sea bottom, leaping gracefully
        A large fish, about two feet long)

There was one like a great sturgeon
        constantly moving and twisting its muscular body

And a fish with tentacles under the fins
        on which it walks on the sea floor!
It has a blue fin, that opens when it swims

And speckled fish, too, with the eyes of snakes
        at the bottom of the sea, their heads gently bobbing

And an Octopus
with saucer-like suckers, a paunchy body,
        huge eyes on great mounds,
blowing out of intestinal tubes,
        coiling the tips of his tentacles like a seashell.

He looked intelligent
Maybe he is intelligent, I thought, like a poet
        or a philosopher
who understands, but cannot act to circumvent clever men.

The octopus opened his magnificent umbrella,
pushed the belly forward, and bumped into a sleeping fellow
Then he went behind a pilaster
        because I had been watching him too long.

A magnificent creature.

And I saw beautiful tiny sea-horses
        with a fin on the back
                vibrating like a little wheel
And a ghostly shrimp six inches long
        light pink and white
and graceful as a star, or the new moon

And a whorl of delicate white toothpicks
And brown stems, with white strings like Chinese
        bean-sprouts, long and graceful.

And I saw a wonderful turtle.

But I have seen fish, turtle, octopus, with dead eyes
        looking out at the world.
What is life doing? waiting for something to come?
Are we all stepping-stones to something still unknown?

Is man, when he is glad, when he is in love or enthralled
        at last getting a glimpse of it?
Are the birds? Are the swift fish?

(Or perhaps they know they are captive. Who can tell,
even a fish may know when it is not at home.)

Then I saw a thin, thin thing
undistinguishable from a twig (just a few inches long)
but on close inspection very beautiful.

Since he has disguised himself to look so unremarkable,
        for whom does he keep that secret form?

There was a light green jelly
        PHYSOPHORA HYDROSTATICA
And a kind of huge one-foot-long paramecium
        PYROSOMA GIGANTEUM

And a thread-like plant with fragile white hair
(They say the chromosomes are such a thing of diminutive
        size, the whole life contained in their genes!)

And a coral that was a true artistic design
        made by a growing plant—
                a Persian decorative motif.

And many other intelligent plants, animals, and fish.

Have you seen the weeping beech
             hanging like a green pavilion?
Or the tulip tree
             reaching up to heaven?

Have you seen the cedar?
The kakee tree, the gingko, the lobed sassafras
             —have you inhaled their fragrance?

The glistening leaf of the strong oak, suber,
       the slender white birch,
                    the dappled maple,
the tough sticky pine, swelling with rosin?
Have you sat on the moss among the brown cones?
Have you seen the contours of the leaves?
Or listened to the silence in their shadows,
             or the rush in high winds?

I have gone to the green pavilion of morning
       and watched the dahlia open her eye.
I have seen the violets breathe in the blue light
             under pendent leaves.

Ah, Wyndham!
Cophetua may still rhapsodize
                       but at the Tate
I did not find Ezra, where he used to hang
           almost life-size.

The beard replaces the necktie,
               the pub gives way to the espresso bar.

And poetry is the fruit of experience!
The present is always present!
                     Ha! Ha!
All you've got to do is be there to enjoy it.

The dead don't care—they're neither here nor there.
Something keeps the world always full,
                     like a daily newspaper.
An atomic ticker-tape?

              Ghost writers?
In a corner of a London museum
I saw the ballet shoes and feather-white dress of Pavlova
               in which she danced The Swan,

with old clothes, torn gloves, and bits of broken glass
               from those times.

And Adelina Patti's tiara—
         a triumph in La Sonnambula—
buried in a downstairs room.

In the daylight of departure from the shores of light,

    the sea was a white burning cloud all afternoon.

    Locks hanging over the counterpane
                                  or grapes spilling
out of the bright horn.

"Light."

    Only in the reflection of portholes
                                  gulls
flash across mirror, a dumb sequence.

                The sea as an escritoire.
                          That pale blue
            and violet
                        heaven.

Like dreams before they begin, a tunnel
        at the end of which a blue grotto,
silently set with shrubs, shines.

Silence, in the glass light of so much meaning
it looks like indifference, and purpose so large
        the details are left to chance.

What I think when I am alone

of the sea, the road of adventure
      —what the soul sees between two lives. Hearing only

the plaintive seagull's infant cry.

All the animals are eccentric,
        therefore we are affectionate to them
and amused.

    Too much of one thing, human.

To die, to drown, to be free
                of everything human.
A clean new beginning, a ghostly embryo.

Whispers, on the burning crystal—of things to come.

In this world, everything is immortal,
                      it merely changes.
A new form, of the same old thing!

That manifests itself in change, even in incompleteness.

We must go.

Where the bios shapes the body, as we shape our dreams
                  out of memory,
into the image we need.

Look at the lineaments,
what are the parts of any woman that please?

Someone you love, or have loved, or will love.

A mixture, that makes things new
           out of dissimilars, making a third.

Limbo. Amorphous cloud. Alembic of nature.

(Why work in mines, said the miner, in London,
           when I can stay in the open air?)

There, somewhere, at the horizon
           you cannot tell the sea from the sky,
where the white cloud glimmers,

the only reality, in a sea of unreality,

out of that cloud come palaces, and domes,
                  and marble capitals,
and carvings of ivory and gold—
                        Atlantis
shines invisible, in that eternal cloud.

An architecture of contradictions and inexorable chances
           reconciled at last,
in a single body.

The iceberg came toward us,
           like a piece of eternity,
like a carved silent coffin, out of the night,
and stood in the shattering sea,
           serenely still,
and disdainful, while we looked with awe
           at its still beauty assaulted
that knew neither time nor change.

Nothing—is always true.
In any crisis, it's the best thing to do.
Nothing—is what it comes to.
It's where we begin.
Nothing—is what we like to do.

Everything comes of nothing.
It "never faileth",
it is as good as charity—those who have nothing
      also have faith and hope.

Nothing is silent. Nothing is simple.
Nothing is left to chance!
Nothing is at the heart of mathematics,
      and number the nothing in all that is.

Les Répétitions

I

Again Violetta's dying.
One would have thought once was enough.

When art becomes that real
        who wants it to be repeated?

And yet we do.
(it's nice to have that first kiss again.)
In fact, nothing is much worth repeating—
        even the sex we vary
                as we do.

"Let's go to the movies."
        "Another cookie?"

The mystical experience is another thing.
Like art, it's something that should have happened
and therefore we repeat it.

(We are never bored
        with something that should have happened.)

"Let's do it again, maybe this time
                it will happen."

We repeat everything, looking for art.

II

What you give some men never get
      not in a lifetime of looking—
                                the difference
between sex and no sex
      is that between your speaking body
and any other woman.

'*Did you find art?*' *she said*. . .

If anything was that perfect
      we'd repeat it because it was perfect
just as we repeat what isn't
      because it isn't.

Alba

O Aphrodite
look down on the clover face of youth
        torn with desire
look at the lonely middle-aged
        without satisfaction
look at the old in their flannels
        denied and played out. . .

Give every man a gentle responsive lover
        —and if more, a child of his own.

Brightness

It is like love, this vision
taking us away from nonsense
                into a great silence.

Youth is over
            joystick, bicycle, the prowess of the body:
I would have it again, but more
            I would have it all erased
for some radiant future—

something it all contains and that contains it
like apples in autumn we have not eaten.